A Body Dictionary

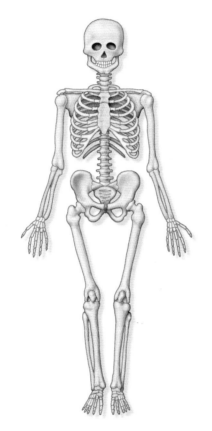

Claire Llewellyn

OXFORD

UNIVERSITY PRESS

Great Clarendon Street, Oxford OX2 6DP

Oxford University Press is a department of the University of Oxford.
It furthers the University's objective of excellence in research, scholarship,
and education by publishing worldwide in

Oxford New York

Athens Auckland Bangkok Bogotá Buenos Aires Calcutta
Cape Town Chennai Dar es Salaam Delhi Florence Hong Kong Istanbul
Karachi Kuala Lumpur Madrid Melbourne Mexico City Mumbai
Nairobi Paris São Paulo Shanghai Singapore Taipei Tokyo Toronto Warsaw

with associated companies in Berlin Ibadan

Published in the United Kingdom
by Oxford University Press

British Library Cataloguing in Publication Data

Data available

ISBN 0 19 917368 0

Available in packs
The Human Body   Pack of Four (one of each book)   ISBN 0 19 917372 9
The Human Body   Class Pack (six of each book)   ISBN 0 19 917373 7

Printed in Hong Kong

Acknowledgements

The Publisher would like to thank the following for permission
to reproduce photographs:

p 3 Science Photo Library/H Edgerton; pp 6, 7 SPL (all); p 12 SPL/J Stevenson,
pp 12, 13, 14, 18 SPL, p 22 Mike Egerton/EMPICS, p 24 SPL/D Roberts,
p 27 SPL, p 28 SPL/Katrina Thomas (left), SPL/Ron Sutherland (right);
p 29 SPL/Prof C Ferlaud/CNRI (inset), Corel (top), J Allan Cash (bottom right),
p 30 SPL/S Stevenson (top), SPL/A Tsiaras (bottom).

Front cover: SPL/James Stevenson (right), SPL/Alfred Pasieka (bottom left),
Corbis UK/Charles O'Rear (top left), SPL/David Gifford (background).
Back cover: Julian and Janet Baker

Additional photography by Martin Sookias

Illustrations by Julian and Janet Baker and David Pattison

Arms

The arms are our two upper **limbs**. They are made mostly of muscles and bones.

FACT BOX

Engineers copied the human arm when they made robots for car factories. However, robot arms can only do a few simple tasks, and soon wear out.

The skeleton of the arm and hand.

shoulder joint

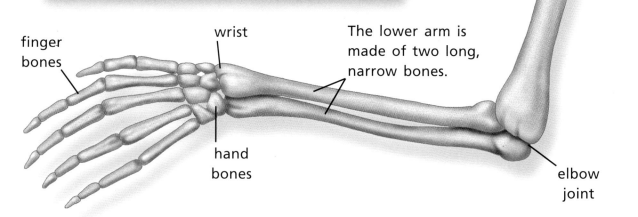

finger bones

wrist

The lower arm is made of two long, narrow bones.

hand bones

elbow joint

The way the arms are joined at the shoulders allows them to move in a circle. The elbow joint allows the lower arms to move up and down, so that we can put our hands exactly where we want them.

Joints p.16
Muscles p.18
Skeleton p.23

Blood

Blood is a red liquid which travels around our body in tubes called blood vessels. Our blood brings **oxygen**, food, and water to every part of the body. Then it carries **waste** away.

Our heart pumps blood around the body, supplying it with oxygen and food. ▶

FACT BOX

We have about 5 litres of blood in our bodies – that is enough to fill about 15 drink cans.

All around the body

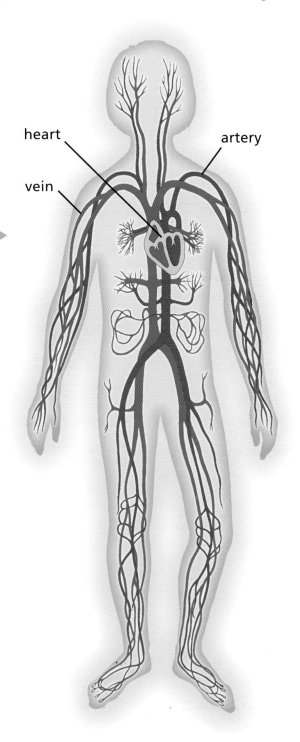

heart

vein

artery

Out to the body

Blood is pumped around the body by the heart. It leaves the heart through wide tubes called arteries. These branch off into smaller and smaller arteries until the blood reaches **capillaries**. These are the tiniest blood vessels in the body. A capillary's walls are so thin that the oxygen and food inside the blood can seep straight into the body's cells. Blood feeds the cells and keeps them alive.

◀ Different-sized blood vessels (not real size).

Cells p.7
Immune system p.16
Kidneys p.17

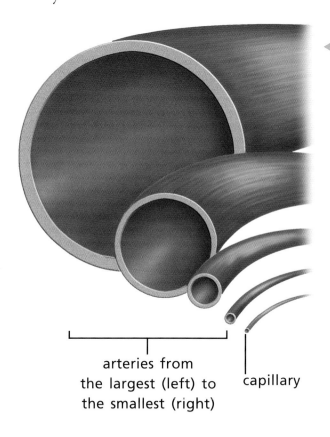

arteries from the largest (left) to the smallest (right)

capillary

Did you know?

Laid end to end, one person's blood vessels measure 96,000 km. They would go round the Equator twice!

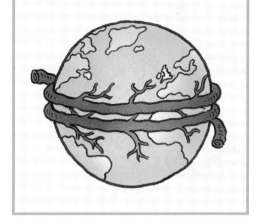

Back to the heart

The blood now returns to the heart. Waste seeps into the capillaries. They join to make larger and larger blood vessels called veins, which return the blood to the heart.

Heart p.15
Pulse p.21

Brain

The brain controls the body. It is made up of billions of tiny nerve cells that are all linked to one another.

talking

moving

touching

hearing

understanding

thinking

seeing

▶ Different parts of the brain control different activities.

Nervous system p.19

The brain does many different jobs. It receives messages from all over the body, makes decisions about them and sends out signals to our muscles to tell them what to do. The brain makes sure our heart and lungs keep working. It also does our thinking and remembering.

Did you know?

The brain is the size of a grapefruit.

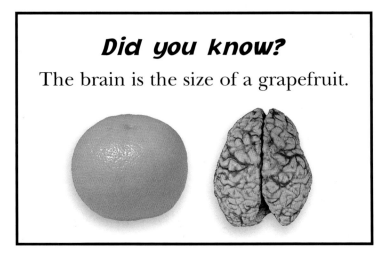

Cells

The body is made up of billions of tiny cells. Different kinds of cells build different parts of the body, such as skin, blood, nerves, or bone.

Immune system p.16

▲ Skin cells

Skin p.25

▲ Red blood cells

Blood p.4

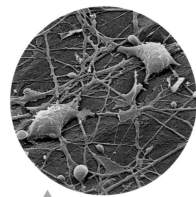

▲ Nerve cells

Nervous system p.19

> ## *Did you know?*
> You grew from a single **fertilised** cell – the egg cell.

Inside most cells is a part called the nucleus. This contains the information that tells the cell how to grow, what job it should do and how to make more cells like itself.

nucleus

◄ This cell has been **magnified** 15,000 times.

Digestion

Digestion is the way that food is broken down and taken in by the body. There are three main stages in digestion. First, the food is mashed into a thick soup. Next, the digested food is taken in by the body, and enters the blood. Finally, any **waste** food leaves the body when we go to the toilet.

The digestive system

Oesophagus p.21
Teeth p.26
Tongue p.27

1 Teeth cut and chew food.

2 The oesophagus squeezes food down to the stomach.

3 The stomach squashes the food and breaks it down with strong juices.

4 The small **intestine** soaks up the digested food.

5 The large intestine soaks up water from the undigested food.

6 The rectum stores waste food until it leaves the body.

A good diet

Food gives the body energy, and helps it to build and repair itself. Eating different kinds of food supplies the body with everything it needs. This is called a balanced diet.

Eating well means eating many different kinds of food.

Did you know?

Most people eat about 50 tonnes of food in their lifetime. That is about the same weight as eight-and-a-half elephants.

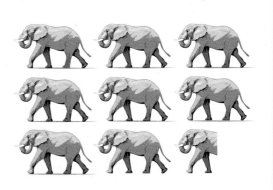

Ear

Our ears help us to hear the sounds around us. These sounds give us all kinds of useful information.

How we hear

1 A sound disturbs the air, and makes **sound waves**.

2 The sound waves enter our ear and hit a stretched piece of skin called the eardrum.

3 The eardrum then pushes on three tiny bones, which, in turn, move a liquid in the inner ear.

three bones

4 Tiny hairs detect the movements and send signals to the brain. The brain then sorts them into sounds.

eardrum   inner ear

Eye

Our eyes allow us to see. They give us most of the information we need about the world around us.

How the eye works

Each eye has a black hole in the middle, called the pupil. It lets in light so that you can see what is in front of you. Behind the pupil is a lens. This makes a picture of what you are looking at on the back of the eye, but the picture is actually upside-down. A nerve carries the picture to the brain, which turns it the right way up.

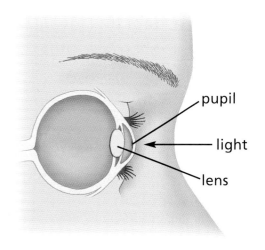

FACT BOX

In many people, the lens cannot focus light onto the back of the eye. Without glasses, the picture they see is blurred.

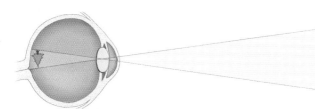

A long-sighted person cannot focus on things that are close.

A short-sighted person cannot focus on things in the distance.

Foetus

Foetus is the name given to a growing baby before it is born. It grows inside its mother's body, in a warm, safe bag called the womb. At first it is just a tiny dot, but it grows so quickly that after 38 weeks it is ready to be born.

Umbilical cord p.28

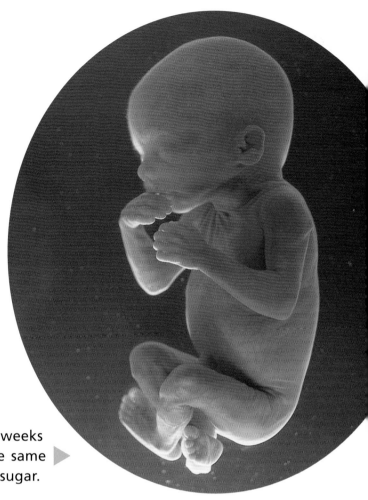

This foetus is 20 weeks old. It weighs the same as half a bag of sugar.

Did you know?

If a newborn baby grew as quickly as a foetus, it would reach nearly half-way up Mount Everest by its second birthday!

Germ

Germ is the name we give to a tiny thing that lives in the air around us, on the things we eat and touch, or in our body. Some germs are helpful. But many are harmful – they can rot our teeth, give us colds, and make us feel ill.

To stop germs spreading:

- brush your teeth

- wash your hands

- use a handkerchief when you sneeze.

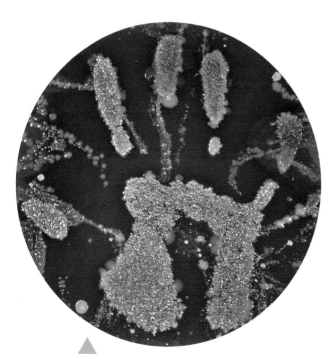

All these germs (called "bacteria") live on your hand.

Hair

A hair is a soft thread that grows from the skin. Hair is especially thick on the head. It keeps us warm and protects our skin from the Sun's strong rays.

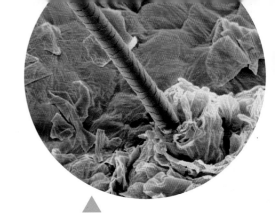

A magnified view of a hair growing out of the skin.

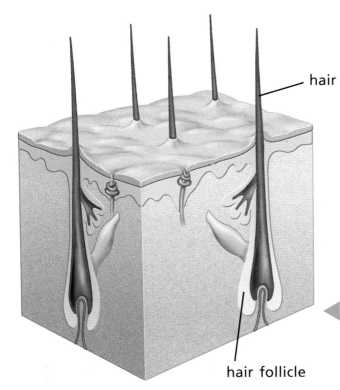

hair

hair follicle

Did you know?

You have about 100,000 hairs on your head.

Hair grows in tiny pockets in the skin called follicles.

FACT BOX

The type of hair you have depends on the shape of your follicles:

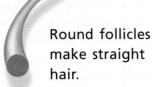

Round follicles make straight hair.

Oval-shaped follicles make wavy hair.

Flat follicles make curly hair.

Heart

The heart pumps blood around the body. Its walls are made of very strong muscle.

Inside the heart

A wall divides the heart into a left and right side. The left side of the heart pumps fresh blood with **oxygen** on its journey around the body. The right side collects the stale blood and pumps it to the lungs for more oxygen. Four flaps inside the heart, called valves, keep the blood moving in the right direction.

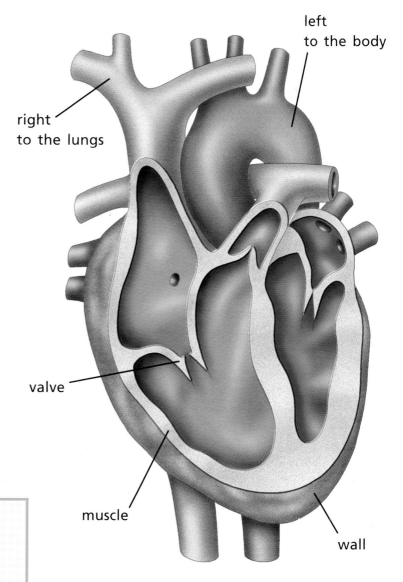

left
to the body

right
to the lungs

valve

muscle

wall

Did you know?

An adult's heart beats about 60–70 times a minute. When we exercise, the heart beats much faster.

Blood p.4
Pulse p.21
Lungs p.17

Immune system

The immune system is the way the body defends itself against harmful germs. Some cells in the blood surround the germs and gobble them up. Other cells produce substances called **antibodies** that "remember" the germ and attack it as soon as it invades again.

Blood p.4
Cells p.7

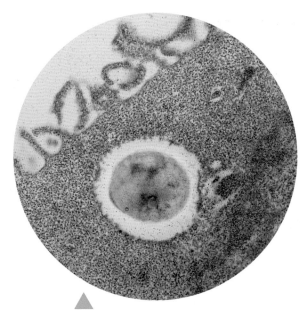

▲
A white blood cell gobbles up a germ.

Joints

Arms p.3
Muscles p.18
Skeleton p.23

Joints are the places where two bones meet. Our skeletons can only move at the joints.

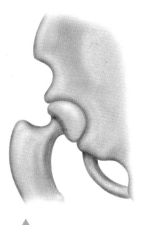

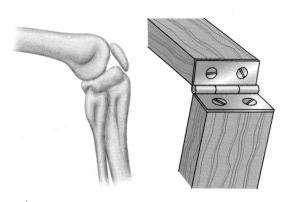

▲
A ball-and-socket joint swivels round in almost any direction. It is found in the shoulders and hips.

▲
A hinge joint allows a bone to bend or straighten. It is found in the fingers, elbows, and knees.

Kidneys

Our two kidneys filter **waste** and water out of the blood. They make a yellow liquid called urine, which we get rid of when we go to the toilet.

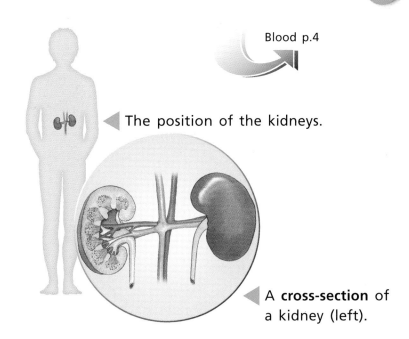

Blood p.4

The position of the kidneys.

A **cross-section** of a kidney (left).

Lungs

Our lungs help us to breathe. They take in **oxygen** from the air around us and pass it on to the blood.

Did you know?

We take about 20,000 breaths a day.

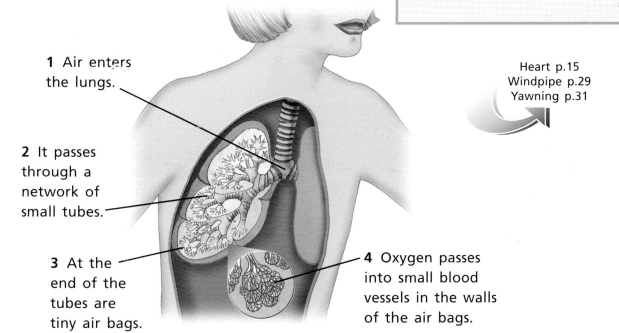

1 Air enters the lungs.

2 It passes through a network of small tubes.

3 At the end of the tubes are tiny air bags.

4 Oxygen passes into small blood vessels in the walls of the air bags.

Heart p.15
Windpipe p.29
Yawning p.31

Muscles

We have more than 600 muscles. They are
the parts of the body that help us to move.

Arms p.3
Joints p.16
Skeleton p.23

On the move

When we want to move,
our brain sends a signal to
our muscles, telling them
to pull on our bones.

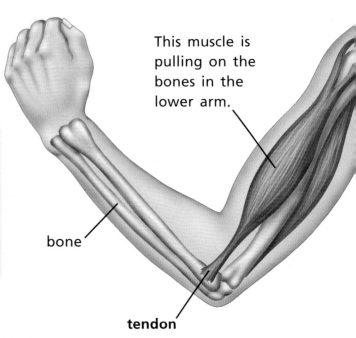

This muscle is
pulling on the
bones in the
lower arm.

bone

tendon

FACT BOX

*Exercise keeps muscles
strong and supple.
Before exercising, always
remember to warm up
your muscles gently.*

Did you know?

Some muscles, such
as the ones in the
intestine, work all
through the day
and night.

nervous system

Our nervous system is rather like a telephone system. It carries tiny electrical signals all over the body along pathways called nerves. These signals run to and from the brain.

Brain p.6

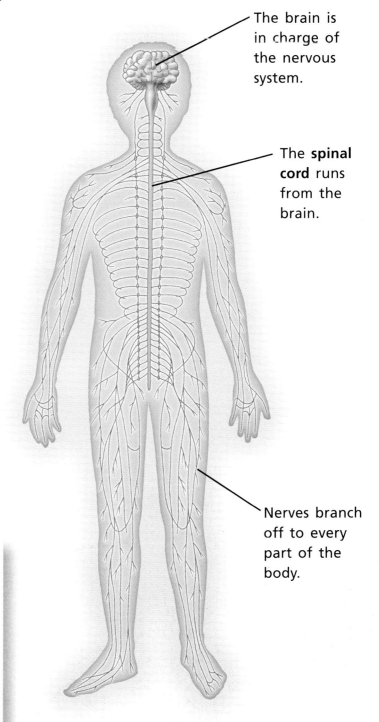

The brain is in charge of the nervous system.

The **spinal cord** runs from the brain.

Nerves branch off to every part of the body.

See over

FACT

BOX

The nervous system is very delicate and needs protection. The brain lies inside the hard, bony skull. The **spinal cord** lies inside the bones which make up the **spine**.

Some nerves carry signals from the senses to the brain, informing it about all the things that we can see, hear, feel, touch and taste. Other nerves carry signals from the brain to our muscles to make them work for us.

Cells p.7

Cells p.7

Did you know?

The fastest nerve signals move at 400 km per hour – as quickly as the world's fastest trains.

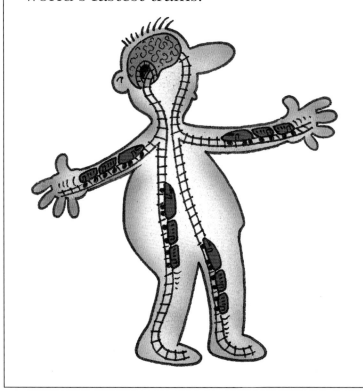

FACT BOX

Our nervous system helps to protect us. If we touch something very sharp, we feel pain almost instantly, and snatch our hand away.

Oesophagus

The oesophagus is the tube that connects the mouth to the stomach. Mouthfuls of food are squeezed along by muscles in the walls of the oesophagus.

Digestion p.8

mouth

oesophagus

stomach

to the small **intestine**

Did you know?

In an adult, the oesophagus measures 25 cm. It is almost as long as a ruler.

Pulse

The pulse is a regular beat that we can feel in some parts of the body. It is caused by the blood surging through the arteries as it is pumped along by the heart.

Blood p.4
Heart p.15

FACT BOX

Counting the number of beats in one minute tells you how fast your heart is beating.

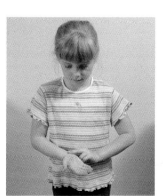

▲ Feeling your pulse.

21

Quarantine

Quarantine is when a sick person is kept away from others in order to stop a **disease** from spreading.

Ribs

The ribs are the narrow bones that curve round the body from the spine. Together, they make the rib cage, a bony frame that protects the heart and lungs.

FACT BOX

Our ribs are thin and springy. This helps them to take the knocks of everyday life without cracking and harming the lungs.

Did you know?

Most of us have 12 pairs of ribs, but a few people have 11 or 13 pairs.

Skeleton p.23

These are also ribs.

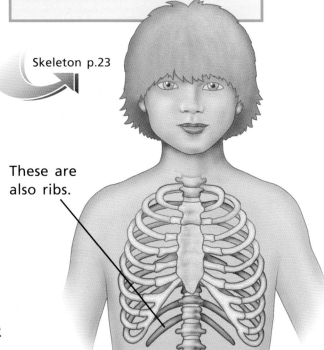

Skeleton

The skeleton is the frame that supports the body and gives it its shape. It protects the soft parts of the body, such as the brain, lungs and heart. The skeleton also helps us to move, by working with the muscles that pull on our bones.

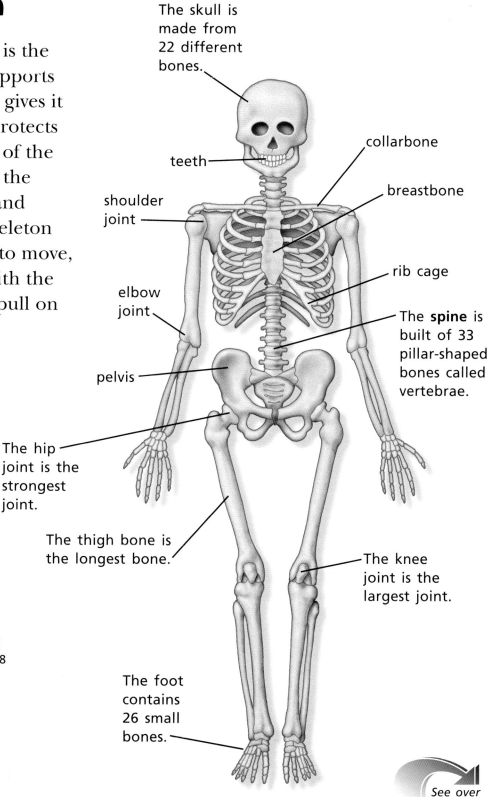

The skull is made from 22 different bones.

teeth

collarbone

breastbone

shoulder joint

rib cage

elbow joint

The **spine** is built of 33 pillar-shaped bones called vertebrae.

pelvis

The hip joint is the strongest joint.

The thigh bone is the longest bone.

The knee joint is the largest joint.

The foot contains 26 small bones.

See over

Your bones weigh half as much as your muscles. Your skeleton is less than one-fifth of your total weight.

A baby's skeleton has more than 300 bones. An adult's has just over 200. Many of our bones grow together as we get older.

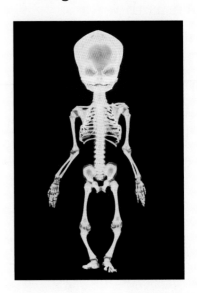

Mending bones

Bones are not dry and dusty; they are active, living parts of the body. When a bone breaks, bone-making cells bridge the gap by making new material. The break is mended in six to eight weeks.

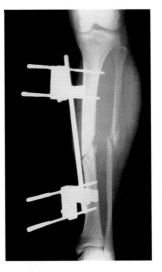

Broken bones

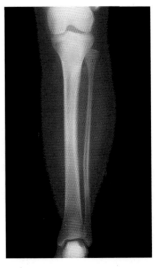

Mended bones

Skin

Skin is the waterproof barrier between our body and the outside world. Skin protects us from the sun, keeps harmful germs out, and locks our body's water in.

Under the skin

Skin has two layers. The outer layer is called the epidermis. The inner layer is called the dermis. It is packed with nerve endings and blood vessels.

Cells p.7

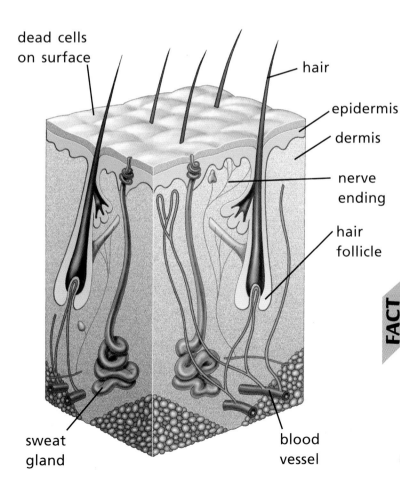

dead cells on surface

hair

epidermis

dermis

nerve ending

hair follicle

sweat gland

blood vessel

Key
- ■ most sensitive parts
- □ least sensitive parts

▲ Some parts of the body are much more sensitive than others.

FACT BOX

Skin grows thicker if it is rubbed hard. People who do heavy work have hard, thick skin on their hands.

Teeth

Our teeth break up food into pieces that are small enough to swallow. There are several different shapes of tooth to deal with different kinds of food.

Digestion p.8

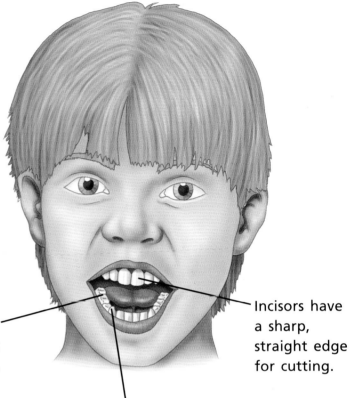

Molars are broad and flat. They are good at crushing and chewing.

Incisors have a sharp, straight edge for cutting.

Canine teeth are sharp and pointed to grip and tear food.

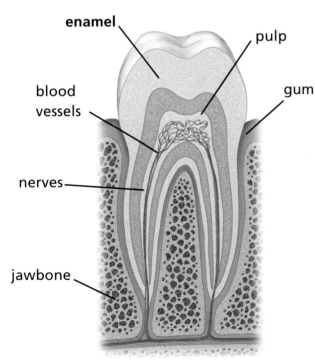

enamel

pulp

blood vessels

gum

nerves

jawbone

A cross-section of a tooth.

FACT BOX

Most babies are born without teeth but, by their third year, 20 small "milk" teeth have grown through the gums. At the age of six, these teeth start to fall out and are slowly replaced by 32 larger teeth.

Tongue

The tongue is important for speaking, tasting, eating, and drinking. It is made of strong muscle. The tongue moves food around the mouth and helps to mash it up. Then it pushes the food to the back of the mouth.

Digestion p.8

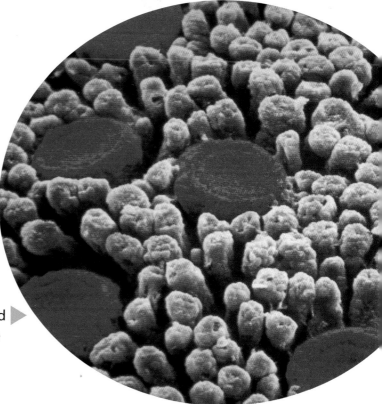

A magnified ▶ view of the tongue.

Very tasty

The surface of the tongue is covered with tiny tastebuds which taste food and send signals to the brain. Our brain then tells us if the food is good or warns us if it is bad.

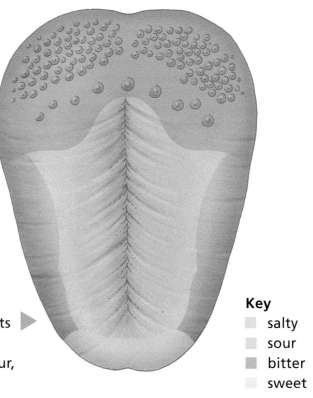

Tastebuds in different parts ▶ of the tongue recognise different tastes – salty, sour, bitter, or sweet.

Key
- salty
- sour
- bitter
- sweet

Umbilical cord

The umbilical cord is a tube that joins a foetus to its mother. Food and **oxygen** from the mother's blood pass along the tube to the foetus to feed it and keep it alive.

Did you know?

The umbilical cord is about 55 cm long. That is longer than an adult's arm.

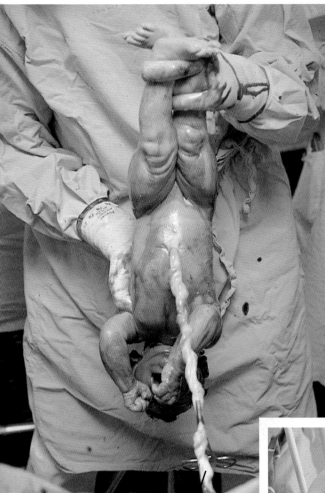

This newborn baby is still joined to its mother.

Foetus p.12

FACT BOX

After birth the umbilical cord is cut and tied. In a few days, the little stump of cord shrivels and drops off. This leaves a small scar called the navel or tummy button.

umbilical cord

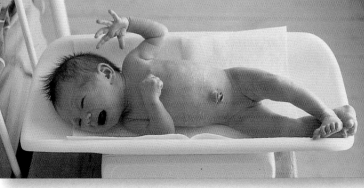

Vocal cords

The vocal cords are two stretchy ribbons that lie inside the throat. When we speak or sing, our breath passes over the cords, which then wobble and make a sound.

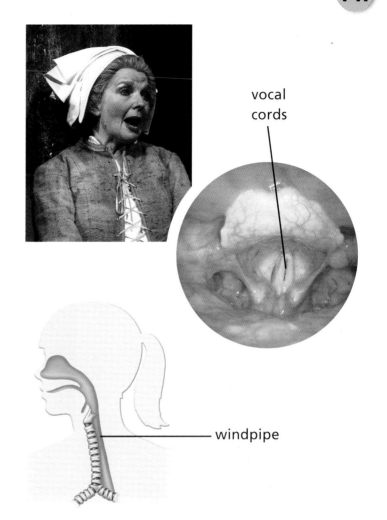

vocal cords

Windpipe

The windpipe is a tube that links the throat to the lungs. Every time we breathe in, air is sucked down into the windpipe through the nose or the mouth.

windpipe

Lungs p.17

FACT BOX

When a person has stopped breathing, it is sometimes possible to revive them by giving them the "kiss of life".

Practising the "kiss of life". ▶

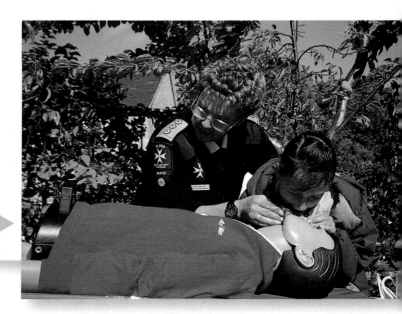

X-ray

X-rays are a way of taking pictures of the inside of the body. Doctors use them to look for broken bones or signs of disease. Dentists use them to look for **decay** or at teeth hidden in the gums.

FACT BOX

Large doses of X-rays are harmful, and so they must always be controlled carefully.

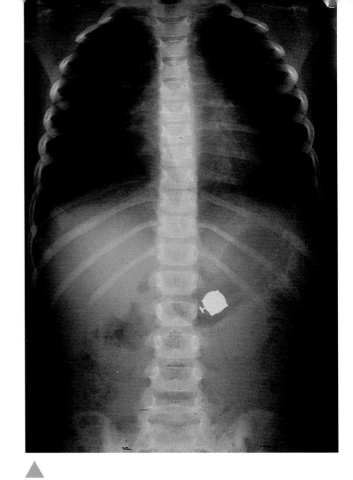

This person has swallowed a watch. You can see it inside the stomach.

Skeleton p.23

This boy is about to have an X-ray.

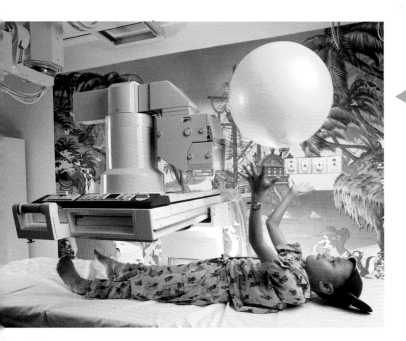

Did you know?

X-ray machines were once used in shoe shops to check how well shoes fitted.

Yawning

Yawning is when we
open the mouth wide
and take a very deep
breath. Most people
yawn when they are
bored or tired. It
may be a way for
the body to take
in extra oxygen.

Lungs p.17

Zygoma

Zygoma is the medical
name for the cheekbone.
The cheekbone protects
the bottom of the eye.

Did you know?

Every bone in the
body has its own
particular name.

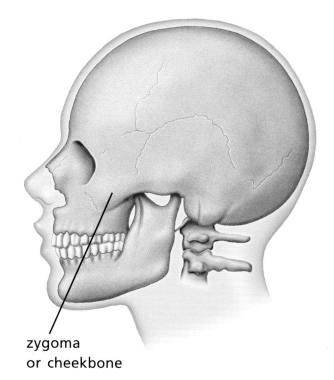

zygoma
or cheekbone

Glossary

antibody A substance in the blood that kills harmful germs.

capillary The smallest type of blood vessel in the body. It carries blood to and from our cells.

cross-section A diagram which shows the inside of something by cutting through it.

decay When a part of the body, such as a tooth, begins to go bad.

disease An illness in the body.

enamel The hard, smooth material on the outside of a tooth.

fertilise To make something able to grow.

intestine The long tube that carries food from the stomach. It is part of the digestive system.

limb A leg or an arm.

magnify To make tiny objects look much larger by using an instrument such as a microscope.

oxygen A gas that we need to breathe in order to survive. Oxygen is found in the air.

sound wave A ripple of sound that travels through air, water and other materials.

spine The long row of bones down the middle of the back.

spinal cord A bundle of nerves that runs from the brain down through the spine.

tendon A strong, thick cord that joins a muscle to a bone.

waste Something that is unwanted.